UPDATE

UPDATE

Bill Kennedy
Darren Wershler

SNARE

Edited by Jon Paul Fiorentino
Copy edited by Lorne Roberts
Cover by Bill Kennedy
Typeset in Sabon and Albertus

LIBRARY AND ARCHIVES CANADA CATALOGUING IN PUBLICATION

Kennedy, Bill
Update / Bill Kennedy, Darren Wershler.

Poems.
ISBN 978-0-9812488-6-8

1. Canadian poetry (English)–21st century.
I. Wershler, Darren S. (Darren Sean), 1966- II. Title.

PS8621.E63U63 2010 C811'.608 C2010-905183-1

Printed and bound in Canada
Represented in Canada by the Literary Press Group
Distributed by LitDistCo
SNARE BOOKS
4832A Avenue Du Parc
Montreal QC
H2V 4E6
snarebooks.wordpress.com

Canada Council for the Arts Conseil des Arts du Canada

Snare Books gratefully acknowledges the financial support of the Canada Council for the Arts.

The lines embody the tensions in the very form of the live crisis in a media-rich society, the question of what constitutes an update and what amounts to another version of the already-known, the paradox of instantaneous transmission of news that will instantly seem familiar. In the poem, this gambit also works to collapse the distinction between sequence and simultaneity–as if we were receiving the full news the instant its transfer began: suddenly, at midnight, it's mourning in America.

– Richard Menke, 'Media in America, 1881: Garfield, Guiteau, Bell, Whitman'

for the We-Plex Supreme Intelligence system

CONTENTS

MILTON ACORN

Milton Acorn is exploring his inner hippie this weekend. Milton Acorn has not eaten meat or poultry since May and feels pretty good. Milton Acorn hates when a recipe turns out bland. Although now a lot of his recipe binder has handwritten notes in it which he thinks kinda makes it cooler. Milton Acorn has a dream. Someday, we won't need 'Organic' stickers on food. Milton Acorn: Your fantasy structure is showing and so is mine. Milton Acorn: 'The work happens where you lose the thread, where it repeatedly dangles off into chaos' (Lisa Robertson). Milton Acorn: What is the opposite of 'art'? Milton Acorn: midnight training session. Pitter patter. Milton Acorn is gonna join the YMCA; please keep all obvious jokes to a minimum. You are all smart, witty people; I expect better. Milton Acorn: Kind of depressing here in Toronto today. Milton Acorn: Because the day of the Portugal/Brazil game should always at least start with jack-hammers too. Do ya think there will be a rumble?? All you haters ... The cup will be ours! Milton Acorn is uplifted. Milton Acorn wonders if we can prepay book orders at This Ain't the Rosedale Library despite the sign on the door. My sense is this store is interested in selling books, not only receiving donations. Milton Acorn: Is it wrong that I like to strike fear in the hearts of my students? Maybe. Is it fun? Definitely. Milton Acorn made a wedding ring today; with his own two hands. Milton Acorn has abandoned the apparatus. Milton Acorn spends far too much time alone.

ANTONIN ARTAUD

Antonin Artaud thinks that dreary Sundays require magical stories. Antonin Artaud *Death Bed: The Bed That Eats* is already the greatest film I have ever seen and I'm only 10 minutes into the film!!!!!!! Antonin Artaud sigh ... I could never go back to the KSW because I'd be in trouble all the time. Antonin Artaud just can't figure out how to get job interviews (among other things). Antonin Artaud needs tips, such as key attributes of a good resume/cover letter. Antonin Artaud is going to the bar to get drunk and meet new people. Antonin Artaud is gonna be up all night doing you-know-what. Antonin Artaud is looking mostly outside his 'field.' Antonin Artaud: New job tomorrow, so I will be able to afford such luxuries as eating food and getting a haircut. LOL. Antonin Artaud On my mind: the very last frame of *Lucas*, hands in the air, triumphant. Antonin Artaud saw a woman get stabbed on Bloor tonight.

MATSUO BASHO

Matsuo Bashōis awake.
Matsuo Bashōis in New York.
Matsuo Bashōis not a dream.

CHARLES BAUDELAIRE

Charles Baudelaire Happy Canada Day y'all, right/on, ride/on! My Canada Day, by/the/way, is monarchy-free: no queen's kings princes Governor/Generals and shhhhhhttt!, can u dig it? Didn't Pierre Elliot Trudeau bring home the M/F-ing Constitution, or/what, Mississippi G/damn? Long Live Louis Riel, Gabriel Dumont and the folks who brought us the Red River Rebellion. Time Will Come! Time Will Tell ... Charles Baudelaire: I'm the narrator and this stuff is just the prologue. Charles Baudelaire was convinced that the gigantic cookie would solve everything and didn't bother to come up with a plan B ... now what? Charles Baudelaire The main thing is that you cram it full of dialogue. More showy, less telly. Charles Baudelaire keeps thinking of music, writing, hobo travel, deep coloured paintings, faded memory photographs, a simple life with no strings attached and little to no money. Charles Baudelaire: Parts and Labour. Charles Baudelaire is reaching into his bag of tricks. Nothing here but a paper clip, piece of spearmint and some old dental floss. Where's MacGyver when you need him? Charles Baudelaire has been stealing imported cars and channeling the money to the president's coffers. Charles Baudelaire This is what happens when they cut funding to the humanities. Charles Baudelaire Got home safely. Charles Baudelaire Yes!!!!!!! friends!!!!!! :D. Charles Baudelaire: Be afraid, Parkdale. Be very afraid. Charles Baudelaire is in gear.

APHRA BEHN

Aphra Behn prays for a laptop resurrection. Aphra Behn doles out headphones, issues of consumer reports, and her own homespun wisdom. Aphra Behn is crafty. Aphra Behn is wondering if the gods ruined her washing machine because they were angry. Aphra Behn is cooking. COOKING! FOOD! It's all so healthy and grownup. Aphra Behn is the type of gal that likes to roam around ... Aphra Behn thinks she honestly doesn't like camp. She's just being brave. Aphra Behn has a headache, and thinks today sucks. Aphra Behn's groveling was only partially successful. Her trip to India is delayed four days while the wheels of Indian bureaucracy slowly turn. Aphra Behn sleep now. Aphra Behn thinks there's nothing sweeter than two beautiful napping children. Aphra Behn is silk. Aphra Behn is out and about again. Aphra Behn has left torpor far behind. Aphra Behn Trout Moss Turtle Mushroom Vulture Shrew Fly Tree Flower Moth Owl Moose Fern Wolf! Aphra Behn's back still sucks. Aphra Behn is wishing people stuck to the facts.

BERTOLT BRECHT

Bertolt Brecht cut ten pages and it fixed the whole chapter. Bertolt Brecht is sampling Luddites. Bertolt Brecht wonders if the people who will vote NDP this election actually think that Jack will win ... and if not, why vote NDP? Bertolt Brecht is now a Nielsen family. Bertolt Brecht is wondering if his kitty would like a sister. Bertolt Brecht finished tiling at 2:30 AM and has become a grout grouch. Bertolt Brecht, in Wesley Willis's voice: 'Trader Joe's chili whips the Costco Martha Stewart's ass.' Bertolt Brecht is drinking hot coffee from a can. (Tossing it from hand to hand is implied.) Bertolt Brecht I don't think I could return to a work world without Office Communicator. OK maybe I could, but it would be less awesome. Bertolt Brecht feels a great amount of accomplishment in futility. Bertolt Brecht is thinking of you. You know why. Bertolt Brecht is bubble girl. Bertolt Brecht choo-choo-chooses you.

ELIZABETH BARRETT BROWNING

Elizabeth Barrett Browning is in Parry Sound, sunburnt, a bit buzzed and melting into a deck chair as evening languishes. Elizabeth Barrett Browning It's sort of hard to know if any Muslim has ever been treated this badly. Especially since the Reformation. I'm racking my brains here. Packing up your dolls and going home because some people might not like you: well, Coulter may be on to something. It's a lot to bear. Elizabeth Barrett Browning searching for a better balance between farce and trauma. Elizabeth Barrett Browning 'I want you to taste my biscuits.' Elizabeth Barrett Browning watched some of Disney's *Snow White* tonight: 1) princesses notwithstanding, Disney animators sure know how to do housework. Gotta get me one of those brooms. 2) animation is wonderful. All of that Arts & Crafts movement woodwork. Elizabeth Barrett Browning 'The cool that came off the sheets just off the line Made me think the damp must still be in them But when I took my corners of the linen And pulled against her, first straight down the hem And then diagonally, then flapped and shook The fabric like a sail in a cross-wind, They made a dried-out undulating thwack. So we'd stretch and fold and end up hand to hand For a split second as if nothing had happened.' Elizabeth Barrett Browning Like a cut down tree I will rise again. What a difference a day makes! Elizabeth Barrett Browning Attention, Scorpios: according to astroberry, 'Psychic housecleaning month has officially begun.'

BLISS CARMAN

Bliss Carman: One of my last nights bartending, years ago ... the CD player was broken and the only vinyl we could find in the garbage room was *Goats Head Soup* and *The Guess Who Live*. We played 'Angie' more times in a row than a crying teenager in 1975. Bliss Carman 30 Hipsters fail to see: Aviators aren't for everyone. (*KITH* reference, for you children). Bliss Carman: If I were a character in a psychological thriller where strangers with the same birthday are trapped in a motel, I would be trapped in that motel with Fergie. Bliss Carman contracts disease. Bliss Carman spooning the A/C. Bliss Carman is wishing for snow. It's just too hot. Bliss Carman Happy Pride Day to all! Bliss Carman is going to hit some balls. Bliss Carman Kate Markoski on Olson as a student of Merce Cunningham: MC enjoyed O, called him a 'light walrus'; was concerned about O's facial expressions ('he seemed confused'). KM: 'Olson's polis is not unlike a dance company.' Bliss Carman runs to the window every time he hears a helicopter. Bliss Carman line: my showing you a picture of my kids, versus you showing me a picture of your tits, doesn't make either of us bad people. Bliss Carman: Still no cat.

CATULLUS

Catullus is writing imaginary words for imaginary books. Catullus Sudden unaccountable nostalgia for the bigfoot story arc of *The Six Million Dollar Man*. Catullus moved. Surrounded by boxes. Catullus thinks the downside to borrowing movies from the library is that you end up watching things like *The Mist* or *Smart People* because it's free and you think 'why not give it a try?' Catullus Apparently, falling asleep to some laconic woman droning on the radio about grey-horned demons with blazing eyes stuffing flesh into their faces at the edge of his bed totally ruins what could have been an otherwise pleasant night of dreaming. Good to know. Catullus Was I the only person there praying to Roland Barthes for deliverance? Catullus The brain coral is telepathic. Catullus just saw a bunch of nude people riding bikes along Dundas (at Spadina). Anyone know the cause? Catullus has just realized he shares a birthday with Amiri Baraka, which explains so much. Catullus would love to publish a book that everyone loathed vehemently and repeatedly.

PAUL CELAN

Paul Celan is watching history unfold. Paul Celan is watching history unfold.

GEOFFREY CHAUCER

Geoffrey Chaucer, sensing a thaw, twitches his whiskers and hops to the mouth of his den, timidly optimistic. Suddenly, falling ice punctures his eye and crushes his skull. Geoffrey Chaucer learned the lesson tonight he knew he should have learned last night: sangria is AWESOME and a wicked way to get drunk in Barcelona. Education is important! Geoffrey Chaucer is the king of the firm deficiency list. Geoffrey Chaucer is not going to buy a lightweight housecoat. Geoffrey Chaucer is getting squirmy at the very thought of it. Geoffrey Chaucer is back in Amsterdam, the land of … well, he's sure you know what Amsterdam's the land of. Geoffrey Chaucer wanted to call you at midnight. He did. Geoffrey Chaucer is copacetic. Geoffrey Chaucer is failing better. Geoffrey Chaucer might still need sleep.

JEAN COCTEAU

Jean Cocteau is remembering being atop the Eiffel Tower. Jean Cocteau will have nightmares because of this. Jean Cocteau at least knows attacking Afghan druglords will backfire. Jean Cocteau Unlikes some things. Jean Cocteau does not want to play the 25 facts game. Jean Cocteau still can't get over the fact that Bertie Wooster is a sex symbol. Jean Cocteau thinks he wants vodka. Iced with a bit of lime. Jean Cocteau watched a battle tonight and, as has happened so often this season, Habs win, Habs win, Habs win.

SAMUEL TAYLOR COLERIDGE

Samuel Taylor Coleridge Giant machines bluntly pummel the asphalt directly outside my apartment. Samuel Taylor Coleridge is opening up three months of mail. Penpal sent me an envelope stuffed with dime bags each a bag containing ... a dime. Samuel Taylor Coleridge doesn't know what to do with these things. Samuel Taylor Coleridge Swallow, swallow, swallow, seagull, swallow, swallow, swallow, 747, swallow swallow, sunset, swallow, swallow ... Samuel Taylor Coleridge Oh Harvey Pekar ...sometimes you squeezed our hands just a little too hard. Real tears for you this night. Samuel Taylor Coleridge is really pleased that Canada spent a billion dollars to attract the world's over-privileged university undergrads to fuck up our city and shout at world leaders who are drafting resolutions that everyone will be ignoring in 6 weeks. Cops need to start shooting now. Samuel Taylor Coleridge the idea of a pleasant Sunday stroll and what you actually get: a passive-aggressive freak show. Samuel Taylor Coleridge has an empty inbox at last.

ALEISTER CROWLEY

Aleister Crowley IN THE NAME OF SENATE AND THE PEOPLE OF ROME, I CAESAR, DO DECLARE!!!!!!!! Aleister Crowley I would like to live in the various showrooms of IKEA. I would own all the bookshelves I could ever want, in every combination imaginable. And Oh! how organized my closet would be! Aleister Crowley loved up his kitty, Charlie Parker, as best he could today! Now he is partying in the afterlife with the original Charlie Parker. Lucky him! Thanks everyone, for the loving words :). Aleister Crowley telepathy float, move in slow-motion as dream precursor haunts us yesterday before we get there. Nomadic of the bird tribe, your soft silhouette, Randall, crumbled with mass as children laugh. Change frequency, (wave-check) asemiotic non-linear flight path clashes park pigeon, bench, 1942. Aleister Crowley who stole the thunder? Aleister Crowley says RIP Lena Horne and Frank Frazetta. Aleister Crowley Thank you, your majesty Queen Elizabeth II. I accept your gracious offer. Now, who would like a tequila shot? Aleister Crowley Giant goopy bird crap about an inch from my bike seat. That would have been awful. Aleister Crowley As is often the case, his apartment was cleaned only because someone who is NOT Aleister Crowley will be in the apartment. Whatever it takes, I guess. Aleister Crowley elects Christopher Hitchens to rewrite the ten commandments. Aleister Crowley: Pixels Invade!

ERASMUS DARWIN

Erasmus Darwin is thinking about resolutioning. Erasmus Darwin cites Joe Brainard: 'A dozen dark red roses in a very tall vase completes this elegant–if icy–still life. A still life with a story. And probably a sad one.' Erasmus Darwin is frustrated that he bothered to get cable. Erasmus Darwin anticipates, and writes of it homeopathically. Erasmus Darwin says goodbye to the bottle of Pomegranate Noir that shattered on the tile floor beside the bed. Goodbye. Erasmus Darwin 1, 3, 5, 7, that is proximate to how I think I must be feeling. Erasmus Darwin is really wishing he could crawl back into last night's dream about Kal Penn. Erasmus Darwin is all out of love, he's so lost without you. Erasmus Darwin is screaming at the top of his lungs, pretending the echoes belong to someone.

EMILY DICKINSON

Emily Dickinson Where did we go that day, we must have walked. There were sailboats with striped spinnakers in the outer harbour. We must have talked. Listened. Hum and chatter: the red noise of heart to chest and the white noise of the city being itself. We walked. I know that. The two of us. Close to the lake. Blues. Greens. Greys. Some sand tones. Yes along a beach for awhile. We walked. Listened. I am sure. Emily Dickinson birds singing, raucously: robins in the maple, crows in the spruce, cardinal in the willow, dove in the grapevines. Emily Dickinson just realized my office walls are the exact same shade as yellow Post-it Notes. What does that say about me?

DIANE DI PRIMA

Diane Di Prima is having trouble concentrating. Diane Di Prima Beware when an Emeritus anything starts yapping. Diane Di Prima imagines a world where all art is hollow and the critic's job is to break in and describe its skeleton. Diane Di Prima is having a hate, hate more relationship with her skin. Diane Di Prima enjoys jaywalking. Diane Di Prima got lost in a Lowe's, literally. Next time I'm bringing a GPS. Diane Di Prima Dad came back to take the color TV the other day. 'I paid for this lousy thing!' he shouted at mom while he carried it out the door. Diane Di Prima LeBron. LeBust? Diane Di Prima wildcats! Diane Di Prima 'Light tomorrow with today'–Elizabeth Barrett Browning. Diane Di Prima Even Secretariat took the whip.

W. E. B. DUBOIS

W. E. B. DuBois is this an example of a game imitating life? W. E. B. DuBois They think I'm playing. W. E. B. DuBois is wondering which Charles Bronson movie to watch tonight. W. E. B. DuBois sometimes writes his updates with www.statusupdate.ca in mind. W. E. B. DuBois is running around all crazy like. W. E. B. DuBois is fool under pressure. W. E. B. DuBois iz w8'n 4 hiz ladiez 2 also rize ... W. E. B. DuBois POLLEN IS FLOWER-COME. W. E. B. DuBois is in the Toronto airport wishing he hadn't tried to get his boarding pass sent to his iPod Touch. W. E. B. DuBois feels like he is walking around w/ a diving helmet on his head, complete w/ 2 Blueface Angel fish swimming round and round as their bubbles go past his eyes. W. E. B. DuBois wonders why the laundry sock gods fuck with him so. W. E. B. DuBois is thankful for all the appreciation for his continued aging process. Also? He is still.

T. S. ELIOT

T. S. Eliot is done with another beautiful Figure of Speech. T. S. Eliot Here it is, freshly printed, the finished manuscript ready for copy edit. (Notice I had to use 2 kinds of paper.) Next week, rap artist Abdominal will rhyme about his sock drawer. I'm so looking forward. T. S. Eliot Pardon my French, but FUCK TELUS! T. S. Eliot is hoping he won't have to explain that a hurdy-gurdy isn't a WMD. T. S. Eliot The Definition is: ' A well-known root vegetable.' T. S. Eliot Laaaaarrrrrrddddoooooo ... T. S. Eliot made it all of two days without eating meat, before forgetting at a party that all calamari were once in fact elegant Cephalopoda. Blast! Eggplant and hummus shall mark my redemption. T. S. Eliot that blasted Ka'naan Flag-Waving song playing on an endless loop in Atrium all day: CBC bad idea #3574. T. S. Eliot is practicing ailuromancy. T. S. Eliot singing the bed song. :) T. S. Eliot Bataille can say what he likes about the Big Toe symbolically, but I can affirm that big toes can really, really hurt. Possibly worse than that, I've ruined some of my very nicest shirts by putting them in the dryer with a ballpoint pen! Terrible, horrible, very bad day. :(T. S. Eliot is putting away the computer and taking a walk by the river. T. S. Eliot can't see the forest for the ... giant anthropomorphic mushrooms. T. S. Eliot is very sorry to hear of the deaths in the Lake District. T. S. Eliot Did I just see Borat get chased up a tree by a bear? T. S. Eliot Must watch.

GEORGE ELIOT

George Eliot seeks truth in the throaty sigh of the terrapin. George Eliot is looking at old photos. George Eliot is listening to spinning tires in snow.

LAWRENCE FERLINGHETTI

Lawrence Ferlinghetti suggests mind over matter, saturation, whole-Ness. Lawrence Ferlinghetti thinking that the nostalgic idea of a tuna noodle casserole was, in fact, much better than the actual tuna noodle casserole. Lawrence Ferlinghetti dreamt he lost, tossed all night (bpNichol). Lawrence Ferlinghetti is constantly winning six dollars at scratch tickets!! Lawrence Ferlinghetti is beginning to arrive places. Lawrence Ferlinghetti is thinking of what realities can emerge from the peacable terms in Obama's eloquence. Lawrence Ferlinghetti is Stagger Lee. Lawrence Ferlinghetti is a bit reckless. Lawrence Ferlinghetti: when I'm cremated, I want it to be by cigarette (tailor-mades please!) Lawrence Ferlinghetti knew better than to go into a Walmart, and yet he did. Lawrence Ferlinghetti is *Zong!* Lawrence Ferlinghetti screams, 'Why, Vista, WHY!?!?!?!' Lawrence Ferlinghetti thinks you'll find the answer conveniently located in his 'Hey, go fuck yourself' pocket. Lawrence Ferlinghetti is a life less frazzled.

ROBERT FROST

Robert Frost is revising something very old and grooving to Tindersticks. Robert Frost 'That is, paper is a thing and it comes from a mill. We, failing to put up with ourselves, use it in our reports.' Robert Frost In a costly campaign of attrition, I have gained some thirty pages worth of progress against the unruly papers of the late Swedish poet. Robert Frost Says I have a fatal error. Out Of Memory. What does this 'FATAL' stuff mean? Robert Frost is about to watch *Inglourious Basterds* for the 4th time. Robert Frost snapped his key off in the ignition. Robert Frost freed his bike from its hopeless entanglement with his wife's bike. Robert Frost is still lost!! Robert Frost needs assistance with his truss rod. Robert Frost 'Could we ever know each other in the slightest without money?' Robert Frost theobromine. Robert Frost's sister survived her latest round of reconstructive surgery and a subsequent infection. She is in Sunnybrook hospital with multiple wounds (graft donor sites) and her spirits are good. She will have another and, we hope, final round of surgery in two weeks or so. Robert Frost has *The Reinvention of the Human Hand* in his hand. Robert Frost 'The wrong wood is green. It smokes when lit and is too newly cut. I cut the branches down.' Robert Frost is only given the option to say 'yes' or 'ask me later.' Robert Frost nobody will own me. Robert Frost is armed with candy.

ALLEN GINSBERG

Allen Ginsberg got paid. Allen Ginsberg spent time in the suburbs today, with my friend's kids, he knew all his neighbours, we had a walk, said bedtime prayers, and read three stories and went over to his new place and saw the dog. It made me rethink families. Allen Ginsberg: overwhelmed with love for his dog. Allen Ginsberg is a cat negotiating the dog days of summer. Allen Ginsberg Cowboy boy band. Allen Ginsberg I'm so demoralized that 51 of my friends like *Family Guy*. Allen Ginsberg is looking for guidance. Allen Ginsberg is playing Scrabble on his iPhone, and loves the little googly eyes that tell his when his opponent is looking at the board. Allen Ginsberg ordered medium but got spicy. Allen Ginsberg has a problem! Allen Ginsberg isn't allowed to use the word 'motherfucker' as a security word. Allen Ginsberg wants someone to take a picture of Richard Munslow's grave. He is said to be the last sin-eater. Anyone know any sin-eaters or sin-eating stories? Or sin-eating traditions? Allen Ginsberg I know it's a marketing gimmick, but Padma Laksmhi writing pornographically about bacon and Christina Hendricks talking about scotch is just too far. Allen Ginsberg haunted by olives in meringue. Allen Ginsberg finds it oddly delicious. Allen Ginsberg DETOX! Allen Ginsberg is enduring the HELL on earth that is SXSW. Allen Ginsberg there is no zombie fun quite like Nazi zombie fun. Allen Ginsberg is mildly astonished that not one of his hundreds of FB friends has had a birthday this week. Allen Ginsberg wonders when his hair will stop falling out. Allen Ginsberg on a mini-moon, radio silence.

SATSVARUPA DASA GOSWAMI

Satsvarupa dasa Goswami is a tightly wound spring finally sprung. Satsvarupa dasa Goswami counted one walkthrough with drink offers on American Airlines, followed by 8 walkthroughs collecting garbage. What did they think they were going to collect? Satsvarupa dasa Goswami is back to work today, sober(ish) and ready. Satsvarupa dasa Goswami sports pink and red socks. Happy Valentine's Day, my friends! Satsvarupa dasa Goswami swallowed his coffee down the wrong pipe. Goddamn. Satsvarupa dasa Goswami wants you to find a way to be happy. It makes him happy when you're happy. Satsvarupa dasa Goswami is researching Gordon Lightfoot. Satsvarupa dasa Goswami is sucking it up. Satsvarupa dasa Goswami really, really, really couldn't care less about the Superbowl. Satsvarupa dasa Goswami will slug the next ignorant fool who makes fun of California. Satsvarupa dasa Goswami's TV just said 'great looking hair is respected everywhere.' Satsvarupa dasa Goswami: 'When black will not be asked to get back, when brown can stick around, when yellow will be mellow, when the red man can get ahead man ...' Satsvarupa dasa Goswami wonders why every piece of art he make looks like it's from outer space. Satsvarupa dasa Goswami has decided to not bother with his small book cataloging all the music, movies, and TV shows he watches in 2009. Hey, it was fun while it lasted. Satsvarupa dasa Goswami damn well would have if it was, but it wasn't. Satsvarupa dasa Goswami wants YOU to opine: Which are the kisses, the Xs or the Os? And what of the hugs? Satsvarupa dasa Goswami is looking for hockey. Satsvarupa dasa Goswami is tried and tribulated. Satsvarupa dasa Goswami sez: I owe you a bottle of the Irish ... and thanks for the pie! Satsvarupa dasa Goswami has become fascinated by inscription devices. Let's hope the kids feel the same way tomorrow.

ROBERT GRAVES

Robert Graves Oh you men of science. I suppose I should be used to such foolishness after keeping house for Victor Frankenstein. Robert Graves 'Frightened Squid Syndrome' is my new term for the clouds of ink emitted by those academics who spray what they think of as sophisticated terminology on the page out of self-doubt. Pity the frightened squid, oh reader, for it is you he fears! Robert Graves doesn't need to hit it big; at this point, even hitting it medium would be okay. Robert Graves Is there anyone out there happy to be groped for a grope booth? Robert Graves likes to have it both ways at once. Robert Graves Since when do I appear in society photographs? Robert Graves substandardization. Robert Graves perspective. Robert Graves would like to take a moment to honour Barbara Godard and a life beautifully lived.

BRION GYSIN

Brion Gysin is off to Edmonton to pimp his book. Brion Gysin: Occasionally I like a little indoctrination. Brion Gysin has a cold. Brion Gysin had to fight another guest for a room at a B&B at 1:00 in the morning in St John's, but came out the winner. Brion Gysin is documenting processes. Next up: backup tapes! Brion Gysin: I will not achieve ALL. Brion Gysin <gross> My Boars Head hotdog just exploded like some 14-year-old boy's acne all over my shirt </gross> :-o ... sorry people. Brion Gysin needs new runners. Badly. Argh. He loves these shoes. He rarely loves shoes. Rarely likes them at all.

DICK HIGGINS

Dick Higgins is thinking in words and pictures. Dick Higgins Of hammered gold and gold enameling/To keep a drowsy Emperor awake. Dick Higgins: Henry Louis Gates Jr. is on *Colbert*. Best academic gig ever. Dick Higgins is ready to kill his computer, but like any good partnership, can't live with it and can't fucking kill the compulsion to keep restarting after every crash! Dick Higgins's boyfriend wants him to log off. Dick Higgins' south-west facing office is hotter 'n a pistol. Dick Higgins has, for some reason, two copies of *Everybody Knows This Is Nowhere*. His 9th favourite Neil Young album, maybe. Dick Higgins wonders why we're still in a recession and Gitmo is still open. Dick Higgins carries the reminder of every glove that laid him down or cut him. Dick Higgins made it home. Dick Higgins minus.

LANGSTON HUGHES

Langston Hughes problem with authority? Why not try turning the tables? Langston Hughes Just realized that I put my underwear on backwards this morning. This explains a lot. Langston Hughes has written 24 pages for two days in a row and is going to try to do so again! Langston Hughes ... what would you say, gulley creek pond stream outpour. Langston Hughes is in it to win it. Langston Hughes is going to see what's happening in *The Yiddish Policemen's Union.* Langston Hughes takes note of the lengthening days. Langston Hughes is writing. Langston Hughes the peace lily goes well against the white bookcase. Langston Hughes: the novel is taking me to jail. Langston Hughes is keeping Madeline from chasing the chickens (the ducks are too slow, the peacock chases back, and the geese don't care). Langston Hughes is getting ready for the Klingon Feast. Langston Hughes can't go fishin' in a buffalo stew. Langston Hughes dreamt once his cat'd chosen the name Bonnheur, and would ignore all else. Langston Hughes is starting to take things for granted. Langston Hughes realizes he can walk away. Langston Hughes is renewing his passport. Langston Hughes has gone into praxis. Langston Hughes is supposed to be writing but is watching for the lightning to strike instead.

ALDOUS HUXLEY

Aldous Huxley was yelled at by a squirrel this morning. Aldous Huxley voices. Aldous Huxley is the only one not making a list of 25 things. Aldous Huxley is reading Bolaño. Aldous Huxley wonders, is he ready for the country? Aldous Huxley has never been tortured for winning millions. Aldous Huxley is baby, it's cold outside. Aldous Huxley is sleepy and needing the warmth of blankets and dreams. See you there. Aldous Huxley is about 8 hours away from shutting his brain down, ahhhhhh. Aldous Huxley watched *Iron Man*. Ah, if Pepper had been a drag queen it would have been perfect. Aldous Huxley loves the politics. Aldous Huxley is excited because the boxes arrived from the printer. Aldous Huxley doesn't know where the research ends and the writing begins. Aldous Huxley is tampering with God's plan. Aldous Huxley is giving one more stab at being a good student. Aldous Huxley is in a shit mood. Aldous Huxley grits his teeth and hangs pictures. Aldous Huxley is retiring from summer.

BEN JONSON

Ben Jonson Reading his car insurance forms after the hailstorm. Sunroof replacement looks like it will be a couple grand. Ben Jonson is drunk. Ben Jonson yes thats a painting i did ium thinking from th 70s yes sew glad yu have it love n thanks b great 2 see it agen. Ben Jonson NS > NB > QC > ON > TO, eh! Ben Jonson momentous cataclysm of rocks wolves were there. Ben Jonson sweat is the new black. Ben Jonson a copy of my book is confirmed to be only one degree of separation away from Barbara Bush. (No, it's not Millie.) Ben Jonson The film studio detention centre is a perfect modeling of an economic arc: the result of free trade boom times and international productions that then leads to a devastating effect on local product. It then sits empty after the business goes somewhere cheaper and is now used to house people protesting global economic policy. Ben Jonson Suddenly remembering that I used to get called 'professor' as a kid. I think b/c I had glasses and read books when my team was batting. Ben Jonson is going solar tomorrow. Ben Jonson *Miami Blues*: Stunning lost gem of neo-noir. Baldwin in psycho mode composing a haiku during a B&E! Ben Jonson took a wood tick on a 750 KM journey. Ben Jonson RAR file revelation of the week 1: Black Sabbath *Born Again* demos. RAR file revelation of the week 2: Fugazi's *In On the Kill Taker*, Albini version. Ben Jonson Revising previous chapters to avoid writing new ones. Eating steak to celebrate getting over a two week flu. Wondering why I keep buying belts. At least they're not hats I'll never wear. Ben Jonson Beer. Curry. Football on parents' obscenely large telly #worldcup. Ben Jonson is now overwhelmed.

JOHN KEATS

John Keats Today's noulipean constraint (gustatory): texts written while the author drinks Edelwiess and lemon on my deck. John Keats Women in high-heeled shoes in the bathroom, mopping the blood from their bare toes. John Keats will be hobbling back to work tomorrow. John Keats I have now listened to all Interpol albums on shuffle and the shit is good. Keep irony in mind plus Sonic Youth and Radiohead and My Bloody Valentine and The Smiths–it's real good–I swear. John Keats NDP-Communist Party merger. John Keats would like to spend some time in a walk-in freezer. John Keats I knew I was cursed! Today a witch-man told me someone turned off my aura with black magic! John Keats every time there's a Canadian on an American reality show they are complete losers. What gives? John Keats Among other things, today is Pentecost Monday. I shall celebrate this by speaking in tongues throughout the day. John Keats so sentimental, not sentimental, no! John Keats loves Big Macs. John Keats Au revoir! John Keats hears crickets.

JACK KEROUAC

Jack Kerouac transitioning. Jack Kerouac what is all this topsy turvy? Jack Kerouac assholes cured me of techno. Jack Kerouac hopes those cowboys win *Amazing Race*! Jack Kerouac the watch store downtown is carrying a line of jewels for men called Bros Way. They are made of light! Jack Kerouac Dear Miley Cyrus: I'd rather watch commercials. Jack Kerouac only just now figured out that 'Mr. Jones' was written as an homage to 'Ballad of a Thin Man.' Jack Kerouac is looking forward to sleep, one of his favorite activities. Jack Kerouac thinks seven-year-olds shouldn't be allowed to use air quotes. Jack Kerouac probably swears too much. Jack Kerouac I guess I shouldn't be surprised that a used car salesman totally wasted my time. Jack Kerouac thinks it's an interesting challenge to try to limit his FB friends to people he actually knows. Why are poets such sluts? Jack Kerouac is at the point where all he wants to do is look at dogs who need homes on the Internet. Jack Kerouac New Jersey snowy evening–homemade pasta and good friends–Manhattan skyline on the horizon.

JOYCE KILMER

Joyce Kilmer is followed by vomiting babies everywhere she goes! Joyce Kilmer fourth cup of black coffee so I can keep working. Joyce Kilmer is going to bed, but tomorrow she is going to figure everything out. Everything. Joyce Kilmer is bored with mediocre books. Joyce Kilmer thinks 'shitty' is not effective enough an adjective. Joyce Kilmer thought more people would be impressed by her Chris Noth sighting. Joyce Kilmer likes a quiet cabbie. Joyce Kilmer is done testing lengths. Joyce Kilmer ... typical. Joyce Kilmer is counting off 3600 seconds. Joyce Kilmer also hates buildings with elevators. Joyce Kilmer makes trouble. Joyce Kilmer just got in from playing poker with the boys. Joyce Kilmer is thinking about Jeff Chapman, maker of hilarious zines. Joyce Kilmer has way too many things on the go. How does that happen so quick? Joyce Kilmer says, send me an e-mail ... I love to get them but hate to return them.

KENNETH KOCH

Kenneth Koch is back. Kenneth Koch is full of cotton candy and funnel cake. Kenneth Koch is apologizing. Open NO WALL LINK from him!! Kenneth Koch is all swapped out. Kenneth Koch is telling you Knowledge is Power. Schoolhouse Rocks! Kenneth Koch has done so many things today, you don't even know. Kenneth Koch is going for cocktails and nibblies instead. It's literally raining on my parade. Kenneth Koch is probably going to sing in the fields all weekend. Wouldn't think that would be difficult now, would you. Kenneth Koch is stuck on dialogue, 'cos dialogue is stuck on him. Kenneth Koch kicks it like kickstands.

PIERRE LABRIE, POET FROM QUEBEC

Pierre Labrie, poet from Quebec's bagel days are numbered. Pierre Labrie, poet from Quebec, laughing at his cat Lowell, who just freaked out over a rat on the TV. Pierre Labrie, poet from Quebec, sings: This is the song that never ends ... Pierre Labrie, poet from Quebec, is hating the snow and the cold. Pierre Labrie, poet from Quebec, is sickness unto deadline. Pierre Labrie, poet from Quebec, is utterly delighted by *The Darjeeling Limited* soundtrack. Pierre Labrie, poet from Quebec, is babies eating lemons. Pierre Labrie, poet from Quebec, wants to be a Flintstone. Yabadabadoo time! Pierre Labrie, poet from Quebec, is doing his part–what's your excuse? Pierre Labrie, poet from Quebec, is recovering from four hours of 1968 revolutionary ideas ... Pierre Labrie, poet from Quebec, is moving to Toronto! Pierre Labrie, poet from Quebec feels the gaping hole today most of all.

CHARLES LAMB

Charles Lamb Black. Charles Lamb found a grey hair today ... next stop, retirement home. Charles Lamb oh no, another songwriter who says 'lyrics' when he means 'vocals' ... oh well. Charles Lamb sigh. Charles Lamb almost hit 'send' after signing a client e-mail with XOXOXOXO while thinking of his boyfriend. That could have been awkward ... Charles Lamb Just saw the *Collapse* trailer and is thinking maybe he shouldn't watch it for fear of going into convulsions ... or running from the cinema screaming that the projector is using too much electricity and we need to shut everything off now. Charles Lamb needs to be good and squeeze in a few hours of writing up the outcome of today's interview before heading out later, for an evening of torture. Charles Lamb wonders why he's never been invited to a *Mad Men* theme party. Also wonders whether anyone has theme parties on anything other than a *Mad Men* theme anymore. Charles Lamb: the room is full of the walking undead ... Where are all of you? Charles Lamb is taking some expired cough medicine and is going to bed ... Charles Lamb: Does any one else still keep a journal? Charles Lamb is going to lay on his couch and watch bad horror all day and is taking bets on which lung he coughs up first ... Charles Lamb often contemplates buying an old car and driving across the continent. It feels like his only true calling.

d. a. levy

d. a. levy is a dangling thread, searching for something left undone. d. a. levy is writing a poem about airships. His horse has an ulcerated eye. d. a. levy been there for decades. d. a. levy: how come no one ever talks about ailing parents? d. a. levy is prepared, he thinks, for the new year. d. a. levy is heading to the dance studio in a black mini and mukluks. d. a. levy is feeling oh so cool ... d. a. levy now trusts that the end of every dark alley is the comforting percussion of double bass beats. d. a. levy hopes the weather's better tomorrow. And everything else too. d. a. levy is digesting soup. d. a. levy stood in the sink and watched dish after dish float by.

LI PO

Li Po: Ecology, not war; trees, not bombs. Li Po grows increasingly intolerant. Li Po is hoping the landscaping is done by tomorrow. Li Po just got two tickets to Radiohead. Li Po cringes over the sheer force that a gaggle of nurses wields. Li Po has an extra Radiohead ticket. Contact him for deets. Li Po is feeling blue.

LUCIUS AFRANIUS

Lucius Afranius is back from hiatus. Lucius Afranius Hello first leaf of fall. You are bright and you stink of death! Lucius Afranius smoked fish. Lucius Afranius doesn't have to eat a proper dinner if he doesn't want to. Lucius Afranius accidently ate a piece of hotdog and needs to induce a good vomit. Tips? Lucius Afranius Dear man who called my office today to solicit donations for some sort of charity thing Toronto police are doing for kids: I am not sure how to say this nicely. You've got to be fucking kidding me, right? Lucius Afranius Dear mainstream media: Not every protester is an 'anarchist.' Lucius Afranius Dear Mom: I know you'd like me to cut back on the sauce, but boarding up liquor stores seems a bit excessive even for you. Lucius Afranius thinks that the mother of the murdered child who asked for mercy for her husband and son has no idea how lucky she is to be in a country that doesn't have the death penalty. And since the whole family knew it was going to happen, why didn't the cops charge the mother as well? Honour, my foot, and feet are an insult in that culture ... Lucius Afranius made a 5-year-old participant cry yesterday–but I got his data in the end! Lucius Afranius OMG a handsome and insanely kind benefactor gifted me a DYSON. I feel like a princess. Luckiest palace owner in the world. PS: Ladies, he's mine, so his identity remains a secret, sorry. Lucius Afranius can't get that sound you make out of my head.

MAN RAY

Man Ray is/was between worlds. Man Ray is fiercer than the cold. Man Ray: rest in peace Grandpa. Man Ray is done but somehow working on client designs over tequila shots. Man Ray hurts when he blinks. Man Ray believes in True Love. Man Ray is starting a Valentine's Playlist; favorite sonnet, anyone? Man Ray loves *Die Zauberflööte*. Man Ray liked Daft Punk's *Electroma* movie more than any of their albums. Man Ray goes through ice cream like a hot knife through butter. Wait a minute ... Man Ray almost gets it. Man Ray is wondering, Don Cherry's suit: festive expression or cry for help? Man Ray is exploring perquisites. Man Ray is an electric powered kneeling bus. Wait for him.

VLADIMIR MAYAKOVSKY

Vladimir Mayakovsky can't get back to sleep. Vladimir Mayakovsky For purposes of a Penal Code section 288 violation (lewd acts upon a child), the touching element can be satisfied by a touching committed out of the defendant's presence, but at his direction. Vladimir Mayakovsky Have you ever had one of those knots in your neck that won't go away? Vladimir Mayakovsky An information was filed charging appellant with rape in concert (count 1, Pen. Code 264.1), rape by foreign object in concert (count 2, Pen. Code 264.1), street terrorism (count 3, Pen. Code 186.22), and unlawful sexual intercourse (count 4, Pen. Code 261.5(c)). Vladimir Mayakovsky Bah! Feelings are the worst. A Penal Code section 186.22, subdivision (b)(1) gang enhancement was alleged as to counts 1 and 2. Appellant pled not guilty. (CT 1:30-34, 1:37). Vladimir Mayakovsky A month after his scheduled release the district attorney filed the SVP petition. Vladimir Mayakovsky needs some new tunes and inspiration. Vladimir Mayakovsky I do not at this time move to withdraw as counsel of record for appellant, and I remain available to brief any issues that the Court requests. I have advised appellant that he may request this court to relieve me. Vladimir Mayakovsky Any day the elevator music at my office is 'Gold Dust Woman' is a great day in my books. Vladimir Mayakovsky He says he was held at knife point and sodomized, and would like to go to the hospital. Vladimir Mayakovsky Wondering how one goes about explaining mental illness to a 7-year-old: God, explaining the facts of life was *sooo* much simpler. Vladimir Mayakovsky If we had it all figured out we'd probably never get out of bed.

JOHN MILTON

John Milton Swedish detective fiction, windy night, rye. John Milton uses some surprisingly impoverished reasoning and highly selective history in his books, essentially using the efficiency of his style to cash in on a thematic without application of rigor, and often without doing his rich subjects justice. John Milton thinks only the shallow know themselves (Oscar Wilde). John Milton is a cat on a cool steel roof. John Milton is slow like a bus. John Milton: a tsunami of conflicting paradoxes. John Milton Sweet Buttery Jeebus. John Milton expects everyone would like to know that today's word of the day, 'splurge,' is a neologistic Americanism from 1820-1830 that blends 'splash' and 'surge'. Also, apparently 'splurgily' is a word. John Milton: 'Some people have never had to struggle. They will never know what it's like to work on a farm, until their hands are raw, just so people can have fresh marijuana.' John Milton recognizes he's still fighting the terrifying law of averages, but continues to survive and ensure the survival of all others. John Milton Art is the primordial relationship of being and non-being. John Milton's blood pressure was 176/128. John Milton is very scared.

MARIANNE MOORE

Marianne Moore before a new haircut. Marianne Moore is feeling manipulated. Marianne Moore has better things to do. Marianne Moore is seriously, seriously cranky. Marianne Moore spends way too much time checking herself out in the mirror. Marianne Moore: Five days to go. And counting. Marianne Moore is reading the paper, wondering if the world really is coming to an end. Marianne Moore thinks someone should meet her at the airport with the H1N1 vaccine or, better yet, mail her some. Marianne Moore is painting in the snow. Marianne Moore has been absorbed by tales of Hindu gods. Marianne Moore is 100 KM winds. Marianne Moore is drifting skills. Marianne Moore would like to know if her students actually know what 'Neo-Liberal' means since they throw the word around like a cheap Louis Vuitton knockoff. Marianne Moore feeling TRAPPED BY RAIN. Marianne Moore is soggy with a side of drafts. Marianne Moore is missing Marshall Mathers. Marianne Moore is REALLY BORED WITH THE REFORMATION NOW (but has one more paper about it to write nonetheless). Marianne Moore is thankful for the Cheburashka, the Hoo-bear, the Kelpie, and the Empress of Iceland herself. Marianne Moore has written fifty questions for you to someday answer. But you must answer with vigor, you must answer with conviction. Marianne Moore is gerunding the future. Marianne Moore is super excited. Marianne Moore is not who you think she is. Marianne Moore wonders if she is the laziest writer that ever was. She kind of hopes so.

CHRISTIAN MORGENSTERN

Christian Morgenstern ??????????!!! Christian Morgenstern just ran out of disk space. :(

JIM MORRISON

Jim Morrison is doing laundry on a cool summer night in Buffalo, the murky sounds of overloud Olympics flooding the tiled room, Brian singing along to commercials. Jim Morrison is taking a vacation from himself. Jim Morrison is also should maybe be possibly asleep sleeping or something, maybe. Jim Morrison wonders who needs leftover donuts from his job this morning. Architecture undergrads? Half-homeless musicians? Anyone? Jim Morrison is always beside himself. Jim Morrison was introduced to the world's hottest wings by his sister last night and is deeply, deeply appreciative. Jim Morrison is craving those soft sea-salt caramels from Feast in Charlottesville. Jim Morrison is playing with his records tonight, and NOTHING shall interfere. Jim Morrison is about to become MC Hammer for the weekend. Jim Morrison: Gone fishing. More or less offline until Sunday night.

GERARD DE NERVAL

Gérard de Nerval suddenly realized, out of nowhere, that he remembers every single word to 'Boom Boom' by Paul Lekakis. Gérard de Nerval might still need sleep.

bpNICHOL

bpNichol Most daring status update so far.

LORINE NIEDECKER

Lorine Niedecker is listening for great Artemis. Lorine Niedecker is looking forward to her mother's preflight lecture about the dangers of mixing prescription medication and alcohol in order to overcome a fear of flying. Lorine Niedecker is flying too close to the sun. Lorine Niedecker, though still enjoying the fog, wonders what happened to the sun. Lorine Niedecker wants to know if it was you who she lent her hot rollers to. Lorine Niedecker is auditioning for the role of Optimus Prime in the next *Transformers* movie so she can pin Shia to the hood of a car. Lorine Niedecker is an action figure with dark glasses and a cane.

CHARLES OLSON

Charles Olson is back ... BLERG ... apparently he needs this stupid Facebook thing to get a hold of people ... and stuff ... I still won't be on here very often ... so please email or call me if you need to get a hold of me ... Charles Olson formatting block quotations: a matter of choice. Charles Olson asks, what are your favourite songs about space/aliens/the moon? Charles Olson is wondering if I'm the only one who finds it disturbing that someone thought to make a Facebook page for Gwendolyn MacEwen and write: 'Peggy, how is the liver? Gonna be joining us sometime soon? Not that there's any hurry, take your time. I'll be here.' Charles Olson Funny what happens when everyone stops worrying about finishing first.

DOROTHY PARKER

Dorothy Parker has taken the Enemy Intelligence. Dorothy Parker jigs, back-trolls, nets, catches, rinses and repeat. Dorothy Parker nearly lost consciousness laughing during *Tropic Thunder*. Dorothy Parker is writing 8 million emails while listening to The Animals. Dorothy Parker just finished what in technical parlance is known as a 'shitty first draft' of Novel No. 2. Brewpub here she comes! Dorothy Parker wants to take herself on a trip–around the world and back–and she won't have to move, she just sits still (Depeche). Dorothy Parker says yankee go yankee go home.

KENNETH PATCHEN

Kenneth Patchen is an INFJ. Kenneth Patchen is immersed in full-on summer in Winnipeg. Kenneth Patchen's neighbours are having a dude party. First they talked about titty bars, then the cost of weddings. The most recent thing I overheard was: 'I know San Diego. They expect to lose.' Kenneth Patchen is making a 48-page chapter into a 15-minute presentation. Kenneth Patchen is convinced this new contraption is a one-way street. Kenneth Patchen please someone get me the fuck off eBay. Kenneth Patchen: The totality is spreading.

PETRARCH

Petrarch ails. Petrarch wants to tell you where to stick your mercury thermometers! Petrarch is half way there … living on a prayer. Petrarch wants to smoke because of *Mad Men*. Petrarch is harder than Buddha, sexier than Jesus and CANNOT BE KILLED. Petrarch is missing home. Petrarch wants to thank everyone for their birthday wishes. It makes getting older easier. Petrarch is needing a vacation away from this world. Petrarch is wondering where the time went. Petrarch's wait is over. Petrarch is in Collingwood.

SYLVIA PLATH

Sylvia Plath doesn't know where the second tomato plant came from. Sylvia Plath placed fourth in the uneven bars. Sylvia Plath is not special or 'special' or any other kind of extranormative. Sylvia Plath Shawn 1, Rogers 0–Now a proper working iPhone, with proper number, and a month's refund with no yelling or swearing or Lord's name. Sylvia Plath is being blinded by the light/revved up like a deuce/another runner in the night. Sylvia Plath is no longer merely thinkin' about drinkin'.

EZRA POUND

Ezra Pound is introspective and grumpy today. Ezra Pound is STILL being spied on by the landlords. Ezra Pound *does* have a new camera phone now, which takes better pictures, although never is used. Ezra Pound isn't cheating. Ezra Pound has been too busy to Facebook.

ARTHUR RIMBAUD

Arthur Rimbaud is at Shopgirls. Arthur Rimbaud is flummoxed, perplexed, bamboozled. Arthur Rimbaud is ugh, hot. Arthur Rimbaud is going to backtrack and maybe try a different path. Arthur Rimbaud is, *you* are. Arthur Rimbaud wonders if you get a mask and cape if you join The Evil League of Evil? Regardless, he wants in.

JALAL AL-DIN MUHAMMAD RUMI

Jalal al-Din Muhammad Rumi has been invited to Prez Obama's bday party! I'll bring the cigs. Jalal al-Din Muhammad Rumi is like a Phoenix rising out of the ashes, so too will you frighten a number of small children playing inside that ball pit. Jalal al-Din Muhammad Rumi hopes that they find their own smell more bearable. Jalal al-Din Muhammad Rumi calls them 'a great vampire squid wrapped around the face of humanity, relentlessly jamming its blood funnel into anything that smells like money.' Jalal al-Din Muhammad Rumi spent the day biting his own neck. Jalal al-Din Muhammad Rumi is freaking out just a little bit. Jalal al-Din Muhammad Rumi searched for 'weirdo sonnet': jellybean weirdo with electric snake fang jellybean weirdo with electric snake fang. Absurdist Semiosis as Irradicalized ... Sonic Dead Speed Racer Monkey Sonnet. Jalal al-Din Muhammad Rumi eats at Kafka's. Jalal al-Din Muhammad Rumi feels liberated.

FRIEDRICH SCHILLER

Friedrich Schiller has a phone but no phone numbers. Friedrich Schiller–caution: rogue robots. Friedrich Schiller is glad he's an insomniac *and* the only channel he gets is CBC ... Friedrich Schiller is listening to Elvis and estimating. Friedrich Schiller likes the sound of a harmonica being played in the dark. Friedrich Schiller is an alligator space invader, busting up his brains for the words. Friedrich Schiller is apparently not very good at crib. Friedrich Schiller 'you mean, live like mortals, for sixteen years?' Friedrich Schiller: now this crossword is nothing but swears.

WILLIAM SHAKESPEARE

William Shakespeare spent an altogether relaxing afternoon at the Dodo Sanctuary. We were going to descend into the Hypogea of Minotaurs, but the line was ridiculous. So we just went to the DQ instead. William Shakespeare: more laughter=less crying. William Shakespeare is waiting to board a flight full of skinny French people going home. William Shakespeare :: sweet dreams here/good morning there. William Shakespeare :: navigating by the stars. William Shakespeare has finished *The Dark Tower*. Posts pending. William Shakespeare is making snow bunnies in the yard. William Shakespeare spent Christmas Eve drinking port with 4 episodes of *The Shield*. William Shakespeare thinks that Irving Layton is a pompous fool. William Shakespeare wonders if it possible to show kindness to those who show none to you? William Shakespeare has never seen any of the Rambo movies. Is this something to remedy? William Shakespeare :: at the still point of the turning world. William Shakespeare :: dusk in fierce pajamas.

MARY SHELLEY

Mary Shelley is learning, learning, learning. And bleeding a bit. Mary Shelley wants to know what's all this talk about being and time? Mary Shelley is giagantor raindrops falling on my head! oh wait ... it's snowing ... WTF!! Mary Shelley thinks that all this rain is good practice for Vancouver. Mary Shelley says, 'Here Comes the Rain Again.' Mary Shelley can smell it in the air. It's slightly tingly and heavy with desire. Mary Shelley is singing in the rain. Mary Shelley is sunshine, lollipops and rainbows. Mary Shelley is wondering, 'what am I doing right now?' Mary Shelley's sweater says 'it's easy.' Mary Shelley may have found an espresso machine for the office; fingers crossed. Mary Shelley is owl-eyed. Mary Shelley is sleepless in Sciatica. Mary Shelley is trying to unclutter her space (impossible). Mary Shelley hates the occasional neo-lib thoughts that pop into her head ... is this how it started with Condoleeza? Mary Shelley wants to live in a universe of 1940s-style private eyes who are fish. Mary Shelley is planning a fish-funeral. Mary Shelley has come to some difficult conclusions. Mary Shelley is wanting, waiting and wielding a very big stick. Mary Shelley is taking time for a big fat glass of red wine. Make that several big fat glasses.

STEVIE SMITH

Stevie Smith sez: That Rita Hayworth was one mighty fetching dame. Stevie Smith is lopping. Stevie Smith is counting the minutes until she can hold her babies again ... Stevie Smith likes Northern Ontario. It's like back home, but with smaller mountains and bigger lakes. Stevie Smith swam with a loon this morning, but is now back in Toronto for a couple of days kissing hands and shaking babies. Stevie Smith says there's nothin' short of dyin', half as lonesome as the sound of the sleepin' city side-walk, Sunday mornin', comin' down.

SOPHOCLES

Sophocles is reading Adorno and pondering his next tattoo ... Sophocles is dreaming Winnipeg, Winnipeg, cake, Winnipeg. Sophocles is really digging the new McCartney album. No, really. Sophocles has one word: Spirograph! Sophocles's code names? Renegade and Renaissance. Sophocles is collaborating on a poem with Rockets Redglare. Sophocles is MOM DAD BOB. Sophocles is going to see art in the burbs. Sophocles is frittering away too much time daydreaming. Sophocles is getting a move on. Sophocles is attempting to follow the brown rice diet. Sophocles is VICTORIOUS! Sophocles is dwelling on the verge of absurd. Sophocles is ... or maybe ...

ROBERT LOUIS STEVENSON

Robert Louis Stevenson Ladies on stilts, fire balls, softcore suntan lotion porn, spacemen and a hangover that feels like Satan is inside me. Must have been a Run with the Kittens show. Robert Louis Stevenson is neither crunchy nor sweet; is the place where the chocolate meets peanut butter; is the teapot in tempest; is actually having a REALLY FUCKING ROUGH DAY. Robert Louis Stevenson another neighbour gone from upstairs. What the hell; fourth since March 2009, and this one barely here 3 months; is this landlord offering short-term leases now? Robert Louis Stevenson considers the full-on Grizzly Adams beard. Robert Louis Stevenson discovered, in the back of the drawer, a pair of socks that I've had since 1986. If you see me rocking a pair of white cotton tube socks with yellow and green stripes, you'll know they're still road-worthy. Robert Louis Stevenson as for my various statements about the impotence of presence: there was an earthquake and I ... see below ... missed it. Robert Louis Stevenson is magically retarded. Or delicious. Seriously, it's about 50/50. Robert Louis Stevenson wrote another fragment of the third novel today; slow, slow, slow. Robert Louis Stevenson 'Just use a bumble enbelope.' I said this. Robert Louis Stevenson: 'until the moss had reached our lips.' Robert Louis Stevenson: there is no dog but dog.

DYLAN THOMAS

Dylan Thomas tried to retell one of your stories but it wasn't funny when he told it. Dylan Thomas is the mystery of the quotient. Dylan Thomas: 'Is the Internet changing our brains?' Neuroscience is the new essentialism. Dylan Thomas is happy that England won the war and that Germany won today's game. Dylan Thomas was measured and found wanting by Stephen Scobie last night. Dylan Thomas was told to go to hell by a disgruntled author who was sent a rejection letter. Dylan Thomas was given a 'it's you not me' speech and accused of only selecting poets willing to play the game. Dylan Thomas has received hate mail before but this was a new low. Dylan Thomas is not feeling creative after all. Dylan Thomas is very very tired. Dylan Thomas doesn't think that poets are generally seen as funny people. Dylan Thomas wants to watch *The Neverending Story*. Fight against the sadness Artax. Artax!

WILLIAM CARLOS WILLIAMS

William Carlos Williams: 'What's that?' It's a sprinkler. 'What's that?' It's a light. 'What's that?' It's the recycling. 'What's that?' It's the sprinkler again. 'Oh ...'

JOHN WILMOT, EARL OF ROCHESTER

John Wilmot, Earl of Rochester, touches Anne-Marie Edward, 21. John Wilmot, Earl of Rochester, reads about how to take care of your rabbit. John Wilmot, Earl of Rochester, wrote some Mixed Message Valentines; look for pictures. John Wilmot, Earl of Rochester, is poking breathing holes in feral cat snow bunkers. John Wilmot, Earl of Rochester, ate worms and toads and rocks and snails à la mode. John Wilmot, Earl of Rochester: the Access Copyright cheques are here! John Wilmot, Earl of Rochester, has 400 red, white and blue shoe strings and a thousand telephones that will not ring … John Wilmot, Earl of Rochester, sees blue. Damnit. John Wilmot, Earl of Rochester, wonders if sarcasm is a legitimate rhetorical device. John Wilmot, Earl of Rochester, needs a cat sitter (no, not someone to sit on cats, someone to sit with cats) for this weekend. Please. Write him if you can sit with cats (in Parkdale) this wknd.

WILLIAM BUTLER YEATS

William Butler Yeats is back in every sense of the word. William Butler Yeats iz finally back. i had 2 change mah entire life. new city. new job. new influencez. new horizonz. new health mand8. and after having a meltdown onstage on da mic ... i knew i had 2 move on frum wut wuz ... i thk all ov u 4 helping me–plz get in touch w/ me–i've missed u all ... WOOF!!! William Butler Yeats fights the power. William Butler Yeats iz a failure az a millionaire ... and a well-accomplished human. William Butler Yeats is sorry for the most boring post ever. William Butler Yeats is depth sounding. William Butler Yeats iz not liking the MacBook Pro remote mouse this evening ... could be sum angry momentz pending. William Butler Yeats wants to talk to anyone who understands this whole deal with putting a ten-dollar antenna on the back of his TV and getting most of the stations he watches for free. William Butler Yeats thinks that being is hard. William Butler Yeats iz writing poetree ... again.

LOUIS ZUKOFSKY

Louis Zukofsky is on the first day of the new diet. The trouble is actually figuring out how I'm going to eat 39 points worth of food today. I cut out my usual Saturday tradition of going to Bramasole Diner, which probably earned me a 39-point meal in one sitting! Louis Zukofsky's book is out in paperback now for all the hardcover hold-outs. Have you read it? I would love it if you did. I would also love to come to your town/book club /library/bookstore/house party to read from it. Louis Zukofsky just got told today by an editor that one of his CD reviews to run later this week was really 'smart' and 'in-depth.' Kudos to me, I guess. Louis Zukofsky says thanks to the *Xtra!* readers who voted him Best Queer Author! Louis Zukofsky's weight loss journal: This week, two pounds gone. Total weight=272.8 pounds. Louis Zukofsky reviews the new Lou Barlow EP on PopMatters. Louis Zukofsky: if anyone wants to see a really shitty movie, a real turd, go and see *Inception*. What a waste of celluloid. Louis Zukofsky is listening to Eric's Trip, *Love Tara*, because a kind old friend gave his a USB key with the entire CD collection he once had but lost track of. Every SK record, every Team Dresch, every PJ Harvey. How am I going to sleep with so much music to listen to and remember how much I loved? Oh look, it's Versus! The Lemonheads! Pavement! Louis Zukofsky: The Flaming Lips equals major sausagefest. I'm expecting Rush will be more of the same, perhaps even moreso. Louis Zukofsky is on day five of no coffee/sugar/salt/wheat/dairy/red meat. I would like to congratulate myself for not killing anyone. Two more days until I never eat another lentil or bowl of brown rice again. Louis Zukofsky *Fauna*. I'm not even on page 100 yet and I'm completely in love with it. Louis Zukofsky's got swagger, and the cicada has one leg. Louis Zukofsky It's official: I have the most stubborn child on the planet. Louis Zukofsky: lucky me.

9

AFTERWORD

Status Update, the website at <www.statusupdate.ca> that 'wrote' the print edition of *Update*, was commissioned by the Kootenay School of Writing for N 49 15.832–W 123 05.921 :: POSITIONS COLLOQUIUM :: at the VIVO Media Arts Centre, 1965 Main St, Vancouver, BC, August 19–24, 2008.

Status Updateis a website driven by two interwoven databases and two RSS feeds.

The primary page of the site, which mimics the appearance of a Facebook status update in terms of colour, font, and expression of temporality, is generated live every time someone visits the site, or hit the refresh key on their browser. The contents of the home page consists of the merged results of Bill's and Darren's Facebook RSS feeds ... after a helpful robot has swapped out all proper names for the names of dead poets pulled from the Wikipedia 'names of poets' page.

The name of each dead poet is a hyperlink leading to a secondary page consisting of that particular dead poet's updates. Like the main page of the site, these secondary pages are an amalgam of updates drawn from our lists of friends via a simple substitution algorithm; no secondary page has a single 'author.' Every day, a second database takes a snapshot of the site, and stores the feeds according to the dead poets' names, so the contents accumulate over time. Each secondary page also generates its own RSS feed, meaning you can follow the updates of a given dead poet in your newsreader, browser, desktop, phone or website.

Like *apostrophe*, this is yet another example of something.